LA SAUCE HP

Lyrics by
JOHN JUNKIN

Music by
DENIS KING

DESIGNED BY KATE HEPBURN
ASSISTED BY FIONA DOULTON

METHUEN

THE TRUE STORY OF H.P. SAUCE

· DINSDALE LANDEN ·
AND
JENNIFER DANIEL

First published in Great Britain in 1985
by Methuen London Ltd
11 New Fetter Lane, London EC4P 4EE
Copyright © Dinsdale Landen and Jennifer Daniel

ISBN 0 413 56390 1

Printed in Great Britain by Redwood Burn Ltd, Trowbridge,
Wiltshire

British Library Cataloguing in Publication Data

Daniel, Jennifer
  The true history of HP sauce.
  1. Sauce — History
  I. Title   II. Landen, Dinsdale
  644'.58   TX819.A1

  ISBN 0-413-56390-1

Contents

Authors' Note

We gratefully acknowledge the help we have received from HP Foods, Market Harborough; Ogilvy & Mather; *Woman* and *Woman's Own* magazines; Rebecca Alderwick and many members of the Women's Institute; P. Baird at the Birmingham Central Reference Library; Joan Norum; Nancy Wallis; Margaret Allanson; Phyllis Birt; John Lomas; J.M. Jones; C. Howden Esq; Doctor J. Hunter; Rear-Admiral A.R.B. Sturdee CB, DSC.

Our thanks are also due to: Len Buchan, Pat, Barbara and Dave at Aston Cross, Mrs J. Le Brun and, above all, Louisa Wright and E. Hardwick Moore.

The illustrations have been reproduced by kind permission of HP Foods, E. Hardwick Moore and Ogilvy & Mather, with the following exceptions: the photograph on page 79 is reproduced by kind permission of the *Daily Telegraph* and that on page 68 by kind permission of the *Birmingham Post;*. grateful thanks are due to London Weekend Television for the photograph of Judi Dench and Michael Williams on page 79.

Hors d'œuvres

'In England there are sixty different religions and only one sauce.' attributed to Francesco Caraccioli

For the past two weeks my wife had been in a state of high and pleasurable excitement manifested by a flurry of intense activity. A wardrobe of clothes had been amassed (quite unsuitable, to my mind, for the small Greek Island specifically chosen for its quiet and lack of sophistication). A hoard of potions and lotions had been procured to encourage or ameliorate the results of lying in the sun. Passports and airline tickets had been checked and rechecked and precious pets had been tearfully deposited at well-recommended, but highly expensive, kennels. But, as was to be expected when we sped towards the airport, before dawn had thought of cracking, reaction set in.

Bolt upright on the back seat of the taxi, eyes glazed with terror at the thought of the forthcoming flight, my wife could manage no more than a few monosyllables in response to my rather desperate, but, as always, witty conversation. Matters were not improved when, on reaching the airport, our ears were met with the announcement that our flight was subject to some delay. On hearing this, my wife's face became devoid of expression with the effort of trying to decide whether she felt relieved at the prospect that her feet would remain on *terra firma* yet a little longer, or angered that the agony she experiences before boarding a plane was to be further protracted. Action was clearly called for. 'Breakfast,' I declared in resolute tones and steered her unresisting form towards the nearest cafeteria.

On arrival, the happiest of sights met my delighted eyes. Boldly printed on a sign above the counter were the magical words *'We serve the Great British Breakfast.'* (True there was some additional small lettering below this announcement, but, with my appetite whetted, I could not be delayed by reaching for my spectacles.) My wife, requiring only a black coffee, went off to find a table while I joined the lengthy queue in keen anticipation of receiving one of our national delights, a traditional breakfast.

'Two coffees and a Great British Breakfast', I joyfully demanded on reaching the head of the queue. Without further ado, the girl behind the counter presented me with two cups of steaming liquid and then, before my unbelieving eyes, a plate on which a rasher of flaccid bacon and an over-cooked egg lay, exhausted between the lips of a . . . Even now words fail me. 'The Great British Breakfast?' I roared. Thin-lipped, the girl pointed to the sign above the counter. Damn my failing eyesight. At close quarters the sign clearly stated:

We serve the Great British Breakfast IN A BUN!!

Now I am not noted for the calmness of my disposition when roused, but, for once in my life, I was rendered speechless. Taking my tray, I staggered off to find my wife, a broken man.

I found her seated at a table with another couple, an older man and woman. 'Disgraceful...disgraceful,' I fulminated, pointing at the loathsome mess on my plate. 'Disgraceful' the man concurred in the tone of one who has suffered much and expects little from life. Furious, frustrated, but also very hungry, I smothered this travesty of a breakfast with every available condiment and attempted to eat.

My wife, meanwhile, was drinking her coffee with the distaste of one taking some foul-tasting but necessary medicine. Glancing at her pale face, the woman at the table anxiously enquired whether anything was amiss.

'A slight headache' was the faint reply from my wife.

'Oh, I can give you something for that,' cried the woman, eagerly snatching up a plastic hold-all.

'Indeed she can,' chuckled her husband. 'Always carries a bloomin' medicine chest with her. Pills for everything. Sunstroke, frost bite, snake bite, stomach troubles...'

'You see,' interrupted his wife, 'I do find foreign food upsets me sometimes. We're a bit old fashioned and really prefer plain English cooking.'

'She's right,' agreed the man, 'good, wholesome food. That's what we prefer. Nothing too spicy.'

At this moment, with the staccato rattle of a machine gun, the Tannoy announced the imminent departure of our plane. Pandemonium ensued as we all leapt to our feet and gathered up our hand luggage. Pausing to check that nothing had been left behind, I found my eye was caught by a bottle on the table. The bottle was of a pleasingly simple shape, reassuringly square-shouldered and tastefully decorated with a picture of the Houses of Parliament. A bottle whose contents had today almost rendered edible my piteous repast, and in the past had proudly enlivened not only bacon and eggs, but also sizzling sausages of every size and shape, black puddings and succulent home-cooked hams. A bottle whose contents, too, by the evidence of their plates, refuted our companions' alleged dislike of spicy food. Yes, it was a bottle of that very British addiction, brown sauce. But not any brown sauce: it was the very doyen of brown sauces, HP!

So the idea of this book was born. Within its pages we have followed the fortunes of this famous Sauce from the beginning of the twentieth century through two world wars, industrial depression and the end of an Empire up to our own cholesterol-conscious times. No academic treatise this, but a patchwork of the lives and opinions of those who have made, eaten, loved and despised this small but endearing symbol of the British way of life.

Dinsdale Landen

WHAT IS H.P.?

Nineteen hundred years of spices and sauces

'Awake O north wind; and come thou south;
blow upon my garden that the spices thereof may flow out.'
The Song of Solomon

The couple in the airport cafeteria with their description of English cooking as unadorned and unspiced might have been surprised to learn of the long tradition of spices in British cooking. Coriander seeds have been found in Kent on the floor of a hut dating from the late Bronze Age, but the story really begins with the Roman Conquest in AD 43.

The Romans 'came, saw and conquered', but having conquered found what they saw distinctly uncivilised. Being, by now, a people very fond of their creature comforts, they quickly set about making life in Britain more to their liking. Magnificent villas adorned with mosaics and marble were erected for their high-ranking soldiers and public officials while amphitheatres were built to house entertainments for all classes. Their opinion of our native cuisine, like those of many in succeeding generations, being distinctly unfavourable, several of their own flavouring herbs were planted here and exotic spices, some brought from as far as China, were imported to these shores.

The Romans' favourite spice, seemingly eaten with dishes sweet or savoury, was pepper. (This is a taste that has passed down the centuries to their modern descendants. A familiar sight in any *trattoria* today is that of a smiling waiter advancing with relentless determination towards one's table, shaking a large pepper mill like maraccas.) Ginger and cinnamon were also popular with them, as were the beautifully named malabathrum, cassia, asafoetida, sumach and spikenard. Among the herbs used were parsley, mint, lovage, bay leaves and fennel, some of which the Romans planted in British soil for the first time. Honey was the universal sweetener and was used with vinegar as a salad dressing. Vinegar itself was used both as a preservative and mixed with water, as a refreshing drink for the Roman army. (This, incidentally, suggests that the Roman soldier's offering to Christ on the Cross of a vinegar-soaked sponge was an act of compassion rather than of cruelty, as is sometimes supposed.) White mustard, too, was introduced into Britain by the conquerors. It was used as a preservative and also served at table, where it was eaten with sausages, boiled boar and stuffed udder. (Sassenachs who may wince at the thought of the latter, take care. Hae ye nae heard o' haggis?)

For details of Roman sauces, we are indebted to Apicius, a well-known gourmet of the first century AD. For boiled fish, he recommended a simple little sauce containing not only pepper, lovage and parsley but also oregano, dried onion, honey, vinegar, wine and oil! Roast sucking pig was best served, he believed, with a sauce containing pepper, lovage, caraway, celery seed, asafoetida, wine and oil. Veal was to be eaten, he stated, with a comparatively unsophisticated mixture of raisins, honey and vinegar. Apicius also suggested several sauces to be eaten with venison, two of which contain dates. (Now those of you who have studied the label on your HP bottle will know that one of that sauce's main ingredients is dates. Is there nothing new under the sun?) The Romans, unlike the Egyptians and Greeks, had no great affection for garlic, while Apicius himself gave the onion very short shrift, declaring it an extremely vulgar taste.

It should not be imagined that the average British peasant gained much immediate benefit from the flavourings that the Romans introduced. He, poor chap, had to wait many centuries before anyone produced a sauce to enliven *his* plain fare. But sycophants among the British landowners, who wished to curry favour with their conquerors, quickly adopted their eating habits. Herbs, previously found only in Mediterranean countries, were cultivated here and the taste for spices was established.

The Romans, however, orginally great fighters, became flushed with their successes, and, as we have witnessed on the cinema screen, began to lead a life of over-eating, over-drinking and over-doing things generally. Lazy and thoroughly pleased with themselves, they were easy prey for the hordes of pirates and barbarians who proceeded to break up the Roman Empire. For lovers of spices and flavourings, there followed four hundred years, which were the Dark Ages indeed, as piracy ruled the high seas and blocked the trade routes. However by the eighth century AD, Arab domination of North Africa and Spain made the Mediterranean a safer sea to sail on and the spice routes between the Orient and Western Europe were re-opened.

It was that unforgettable date, 1066, and the Norman Conquest that really started the gastric juices flowing in Britain once again. The Normans brought with them an even greater range of spices than the Romans. Cinnamon, ginger, mace, cloves, grains of paradise, saffron, cardamom, nutmegs and galingale (a type of ginger, prized for its digestive properties) were all enthusiastically received. Not only the very rich used them, but also the smaller landlords and minor gentry. These spices had usually travelled overland from the distant Orient via Arabia to the ports of the East Mediterranean, and from there to the Italian ports of Venice and Genoa. Venetian merchants grew rich on the profits of the spice trade and as full-bellied as the sails of their galleys, which travelled to London, Southampton and Rochester until the fifteenth century. Spices were also brought back to Britain by men returning from the Crusades, who, if originally inspired by religious zeal, were not above using their travels for material advantage.

The purity of spices imported into Britain was often suspect, as substances of a decidedly dubious nature were often added to make up the required weight. To establish standards of purity, therefore, and to oversee the trade, the Guild of Pepperers was established in London, the centre of the British spice trade, by the twelfth century. For those of you who may have been accused of 'garbled speech' after a drink or two, it may be of interest to know that a 'garbler' was originally an employee of the Guild of Pepperers. His job it was to check the purity of the spices and throw away any rubbish they might contain!

The taste for spices was such that mediaeval landlords would

often accept them in lieu of money for rents. (Hence the term 'peppercorn rent'.) Heavy spicing certainly improved fish and meat that was less than fresh, but, through regular consumption, a liking for it developed unconnected with such mundane considerations. The fish and meat dishes consumed by the prosperous contained flavourings in abundance. The ingredients of a recipe for stewed beef could contain cinnamon, cloves, mace, grains of paradise, onions, parsley, sage, saffron, salt and vinegar.

Nowadays, one is proud of the mint, parsley and chives growing in one's window box, but such plants pale into insignificance beside the contents of a mediaeval herb garden. There one might not only have found native British herbs, but also coriander, fennel, cumin, dill, peony, aniseed, caraway and liquorice. The lady of the manor kept the key to the cupboard (a small pantry), where her precious hoard of spices was stored. As the key was usually secreted about her person, physical assault would have been necessary to wrest it from her.

Amongst the poorer people, pepper, peony seed, garlic and fennel seed were used, as well as the cheapest of home-grown spices, mustard. Mustard was eaten with everything, and in the context of this book it is interesting to find that, although usually made at home, for festive occasions it was often obtained from professional sauce makers. The appetite for sauces grew apace, so that, by the time of Elizabeth I, the money spent on a 'subtle' sauce for roasted swan would have kept a poor family in food for a year.

By the Elizabethan age, however, control of the spice trade had been taken away from the Venetians. In 1498, Vasco da Gama, the Portuguese explorer, sailed into the Port of Calcutta. With his discovery of the sea route to the Indies, spices no longer needed to be brought to Europe overland from the East. The Portuguese now controlled the European spice trade for about a century, and were superseded in their turn by the Dutch.

The British were not slow off the mark, however. In 1600, a charter was granted to a number of merchants, styling themselves the British East India Company, which enabled them to sail to the East Indies for the purposes of trade. So precious were the spices considered that they were paid for in gold, silver and looking-glasses, and the men employed to unload the cargoes were provided with suits without pockets. Samuel Pepys graphically described the spice-laden hold of one of the 'Indian' ships moored at London. 'The greatest wealth lie [sic] in confusion that a man can see in the world — pepper scattered through every chink, you trod upon it, and in cloves and nutmegs I walked about the knees — whole rooms full.'

Gradually the British East India Company gained ascendancy over the Dutch and became a force to be reckoned with. It progressed from a trading to a military force, eventually colonising India. It could be said, therefore, that our love of spices led us to acquiring the jewel in our Imperial Crown.

By the second half of the eighteenth century, spices were available from other sources. Capsicums and vanilla were brought back from South America, and allspice from the British West Indies. With a wide range of spices to choose from at reasonable prices, the British began to use them with more discretion than their heavy-handed ancestors. Their love for strong flavouring was now satisfied by the pickles and chutneys brought back by the East India merchants. Kitchens in the houses of the gentry became hives of activity as red-faced cooks attempted to pickle cucumbers, melon, onions and peaches to taste like mangoes. (Whether they tasted like mangoes is debatable, but the results as handed down to us today are delicious. Dinsdale's great Aunt Mona has had to be physically restrained from purchasing the entire range of home-made pickles and chutneys for sale at the Women's Institute stall at her local market.)

The pickling liquor, originally used to preserve fruit or vegetables was now either used as a sauce in its own right or as a piquant addition to a made-up dish. By the late eighteenth century 'store sauces' were beginning to be found on the shelves of well-stocked larders. These were based on the sauces used by the ships of the East India Company to relieve the monotony of the fare on a long sea-voyage. Based on combinations of vinegar, horse radish, soy, garlic, pickled walnuts, oysters, cockles, mushrooms, lemons, anchovies and onions, they sound explosive enough to revive the most jaded of palates. By the mid-nineteenth century hundreds of British store cupboards smugly displayed their own family version of such sauces or 'catsups'.

But while the cooks of the gentry and the monied middle classes busily potted their pickles, cooked their chutneys and stirred their sauces, what about the poorer members of society? They, above all others, had need of something to enliven their monotonous diet. Lack of money meant that even the humble pickled onion and red cabbage were luxuries to be indulged in only at Christmas. In the expanding industrial towns of Victorian

Britain exhausted women, working in the new factories and attempting to bring up large families, had neither the time, space or equipment needed to pickle and preserve. A commercially-produced sauce, at a price the masses could afford, was sorely needed.

Sauces had begun to be produced commercially in the late eighteenth century, Lazenby's and Harvey's being two of the most successful. In 1823, a Mr Lea and a Mr Perrins, chemists and druggists, set up in business in Worcester as wholesalers and retailers of pharmaceuticals, toiletries and groceries. One day amongst the medicines and hair pomades in their prospering emporium, there appeared Lord Marcus Sandys, ex Governor of Bengal. He had in his hand a recipe for a sauce he had greatly enjoyed whilst in India and requested Messrs Lea and Perrins to make it up for him. They readily obliged, making up a quantity both for his lordship and for themselves. On tasting the latter, the two chemists were nearly catapulted through their roof with shock. This was surely none other than liquid gunpowder! Murmuring darkly about the eccentric tastes of the British aristocracy, they consigned the remaining jars to the cellars and intended oblivion. Some time later, however, before disposing of these jars, they courageously decided to retaste the contents. Wonder of wonders, these had now matured into a sauce of a rare piquancy. The recipe was hastily purchased from Lord Sandys and in 1838 one of the most famous English sauces was launched commercially. Later in the century other sauces appeared on the market, under such proudly imperial labels as 'Nabob', 'Mandarin', and 'Empress of India'. But these sauces reached a largely middle-class public and the great British popular sauce had yet to be produced. Where was the man who would bring this delight into the drab lives of the remainder of the population?

He was found in the heart of industrial Britain and yet within easy reach of the birthplace of William Shakespeare. A man of his time, honest, sober, fond of a good sermon and yet energetic, ambitious, quick to seize an opportunity and with the ability to drive a hard bargain. His business was situated on land mentioned in the Domesday Book. Land on which had been built one of the most important English country houses, Aston Hall, which had entertained a king and been the scene of fighting during the Civil War. On this land also had now been established what was to be one of the most famous football clubs in the nation. Moreover in one of the streets of small houses nearby, Arthur Conan Doyle, the creator of the most famous detective in English fiction, had practised his profession as a doctor.

How could such a background, so impeccably British, fail to produce a sauce that would tickle the palate of the nation and become part of its way of life?

The birthplace of HP Sauce

The manor of Aston, mentioned in the Domesday Book, had been in the possession of the Holte family since the twelfth century. Its most notorious member had been one Thomas Holte, created a baronet in 1611, and a man of a somewhat impatient nature. Indeed when his previously much-praised cook had the misfortune one day to be less than prompt with the serving of dinner, it is reputed that Sir Thomas picked up a cleaver and split the poor man's head in twain.

To the credit of this somewhat impetuous character, it must be said that he caused to be built one of the most important of Jacobean country houses, Aston Hall. Sir Thomas was a staunch Royalist and is believed to have entertained Charles I at the Hall in 1642. During the Civil War, a large presence of Royalist troops was stationed at Aston Hall, which much enraged the Parliamentarians of nearby 'Bromwicham' (modern-day Birmingham). Fierce fighting broke out between the two sides and the damage done to the great staircase of the Hall is still visible today.

The house passed out of the ownership of the Holte family in the early nineteenth century but its last tenant also bore a distinguished name: James Watt, son of the great engineer. After his death, it was bought by a private company, which persuaded

Queen Victoria to lend her august presence to its official opening to the public. Shortly after this, Birmingham Corporation acquired the land for use as a public park and the Hall as a museum. Much of the original parkland was sold off as building sites, the initial development consisting of imposingly desirable residences for the middle classes.

These were followed in time by smaller tunnel-back villas built for the skilled craftsmen who worked in neighbouring Birmingham. But the last and largest development was of small back-to-back cottages of the *Coronation Street* variety, intended for the workforce required by the growth of local industries.

In 1851, Aston Manor had a population of a mere 6,426 and even in the 1870s there were large tracts of open land still visible, but by the 1880s the population had increased tenfold.

Two events of great future significance occurred in this proudly independent borough in the early 1870s. Firstly, a local Wesleyan chapel founded a football club that gave birth to the great name of Aston Villa. The second occurrence was the arrival of an ambitious young man, lately a representative of Pinks Pickles of Portsmouth, now seeking to establish his own business. He had been drawn to the neighbourhood by the availability of cheap labour but even more by the abundant local supply of hard water.

Hard water is vital to brewing industries and, to the disgust of the Temperance Societies, several brewers of ale established their factories at Aston, including Ansells. But if hard water was essential to the brewing of ale, it was no less so to the brewing of vinegar. And so it came to pass that this young man, known as Edwin Samson Moore, established his Midland Vinegar Company at Tower Road, Aston Cross, in 1875.

Edwin Samson Moore, energetic and outgoing, was in his mid-twenties and possessed many of the qualities admired by the Victorians. He had a great respect for George Dawson, a well-known Nonconformist minister. In one of his sermons to the working classes, Dawson had thundered, 'The reason class legislation has been so long dominant is that people have been too much bemuddled with drink to interfere.'

'Bemuddled with drink' Moore certainly was not. He appreciated the occasional tot of whisky, but was otherwise abstemious

Edwin Samson Moore centre *on a shooting party*

and preferred his employees to be of a similar persuasion. He was prepared to work hard to achieve his ambitions and to this end he moved his family from a pleasant suburb to a house adjacent to the brewery. His wife, Mary, had gently protested against living in an atmosphere permeated with the smell of vinegar but had been firmly, if politely, overruled. (She may have disliked the smell but it did little to affect the robustness of her health and she proceeded to produce the large family typical of the period.)

Edwin was a man of high principles, but he was also a businessman and not above a little harmless opportunism. He was in the process of inducing his cousin Edward Eastwood (himself a cousin of the famous railway engineer Thomas Telford) to invest in the Midland Vinegar Company when Mary gave birth to their first son. The child was promptly named Edwin Eastwood Moore and the cousin asked to become a godfather. Duly flattered, Edward Eastwood readily accepted and also provided the necessary financial backing for the new company. (As there are now two Edwins in the story, the father will from now on be referred to as Samson — a name in any case not inappropriate for one of strong character — although we can promise no Delilah!)

With his finances secure and his family settled, Samson took his first steps on the road to success. The smell of vinegar began to mingle with that coming from the neighbouring maltsters, Ansells. The result was unique and became a distinguishing feature of Aston Cross, remembered by residents and visitors alike — sometimes with distaste, sometimes with affection, but always remembered.

There were other well-established vinegar brewers in the locality and someone of fainter heart might have doubted the wisdom of adding yet another to their number, but Samson was undaunted. The demand for vinegar was increasing. Chipped potatoes, recently introduced from France, were becoming very popular when eaten with fried fish. This already succulent dish could be even further improved, he maintained, by a hefty sprinkling of vinegar.

Samson also took up the agencies for such useful products as jelly crystals, custard powder, coffee essence and gravy browning, and began to bottle his own pickles. As a result the Midland Vinegar Company was now the centre of intense activity. The vinegar brewery employed most of the inhabitants of the surrounding terraced houses and, more often than not, several members of the same family. (In such a situation it became increasingly difficult to criticise any member of the workforce as the man standing next to you would invariably turn out to be his brother-in-law!)

These busy employees were greatly saddened by a tragedy that occurred to two of their number in 1883. James Huddlestone and Thomas Wilkins had been life-long friends and worked side by side at the brewery. One day an accident occurred in which both men were drowned in a vat of vinegar. Their joint headstone in a local graveyard bears the touching inscription 'In their death they were not divided'.

Samson Moore's business continued to thrive. In 1890, his elder son, the gentle featured 'Eddie' Moore joined the firm. So, too, in 1893 did his daughter Minnie, although not without parental opposition. Having learnt to type, Minnie was eager to practise her skill by working for her father's company, but Samson was no great advocate of women's emancipation and Mary feared for the modesty of her daughter. Eventually they agreed to her request on the understanding that she accepted two conditions.

One, that she should work under her father's supervision and, two, that she should be screened from public gaze. Minnie willingly complied and typed happily away in her seclusion.

With the invaluable help of his son, Samson's business prospered as never before. He was now the proud owner of impressive York Lodge in the pleasant suburb of Erdington and, in short, presented the perfect picture of prosperity. But he was a man of great ambition and energy and there was one goal, above all, he still desired to achieve.

Grave of James Huddleston and
Thomas Wilkins

The wedding of Edwin Eastwood Moore (1907)
seated left *Mary Moore*, right *Edith Mary Hardwick;*
the men standing left *Edwin Samson Moore*
right *Edwin Eastwood Moore*

Mr Moore achieves his ambition and HP Sauce is launched upon a grateful world

Samson still had a dream unfulfilled. Using the expertise acquired in the vinegar and pickle trades, he aspired to manufacture a sauce that would become a household name. He knew the time was ripe for such a venture. Spices were cheaper owing to the expansion of trade, and railways and canals had made the farthest parts of the country accessible.

The meals of the well-to-do in late Victorian England, though of gargantuan size by today's standards, were bland compared to those of their forefathers. Their food had begun to acquire the pallor beloved by the Edwardians in their decor and complexions. Further down the social scale, where cleanliness was considered next to godliness, 'plain, wholesome food' was the ideal (an attitude shared by the all-powerful nannies ruling over the nurseries of the children of the rich). The diet of the poor, limited by low wages, was monotonous in the extreme. In all cases, some colour and flavouring would be welcome.

Mary Moore was given no time to relax amongst the antimacassars and aspidistras of her new home, but was busily employed testing countless sauce recipes. Stirring and tasting she may well have had the words of Mrs Beeton ringing in her ears. 'The preparation and appearance of sauces... are of the highest consequence. Their special adaptability to the various viands they are to accompany cannot be too much studied, in order that they may harmonise and blend with them as perfectly... as does a pianoforte accompaniment with the voice of the singer!' A tall order indeed and one that, as yet, poor Mary seemed to have little hope of fulfilling. Samson, too, had his problems. For if Mary had so far failed to find the right recipe, so Samson had failed to find the right name. It was essential that a name be found for his sauce — both eye-catching and easy to remember. As if to reward their hard labour, a good fairy appeared, in the guise of a bad debt, to provide the solution to both problems.

As well as the quest for his sauce and its name, Samson was also occupied with all the usual worries of running a business. Amongst these was the tardy payment of accounts. One of the small grocers' shops that was in arrears belonged to Mr F. G. Garton of Nottingham. Mr Garton's debt was probably due to the poverty of the shop's locality, for he himself worked hard to make a living. By day he and his wife toiled in their general store, while in the evenings, tired as he was, he trundled round the streets of Nottingham with a basket cart loaded with supplies of groceries and of his home-made sauce.

Samson and Eddie, finding themselves in the vicinity of Mr Garton's shop one day, decided that a personal visit might succeed where notes of reminder had failed. Entering the store, they were met by a shamefaced Mr Garton. But Samson, though a keen man of business, was no ogre and tactfully suggested they talked in the back of the premises, away from any curious customers. Mrs Garton was bidden to mind the shop and the Moores were ushered to the rear of the building. Here, in a washhouse copper, a sauce was brewing, a sauce that smelled uncommonly good. It promised to fulfill Mrs Beeton's dictum that a sauce should not be 'too piquant on the one hand, or too mawkish on the other'.

Suddenly, Samson's attention was caught by a small basket cart standing lopsidedly in the yard. In a blinding moment of revelation he knew that his quest was at an end. Attached to the basket cart was a board, bearing, in clumsily painted letters, the magic words 'Garton's HP Sauce'! Simple and arresting, it was all that Samson had been looking for in a name. When asked for an explanation of the letters 'HP', Mr Garton replied that

top *Edwin Eastwood Moore leaving for work
in the morning;*
below *Edwin Samson Moore*

he had heard a faint rumour that a bottle of his sauce had been seen in a restaurant at the Houses of Parliament.

Samson's excitement knew no bounds. The Houses of Parliament! What more appropriate symbol could be found for a sauce of national appeal? Within minutes, Mr Garton's debt had been cancelled and £150 paid for the name and recipe for his sauce. The jubilant Moores departed for Aston, where a week later the little basket cart also arrived, having travelled by train. Mr Garton himself leaves our story. Did he, one wonders, regret lacking the means to exploit the potential of his own sauce? Or did he perhaps bask in self-reflected glory on seeing his name prominently displayed on the soon-to-be-famous bottles?

Meanwhile the sagacious Samson was handling his new acquisition with all the care of a racehorse trainer preparing a promising colt for his first race. Until the conditions and timing for the launch of the Sauce were absolutely right, he would bide his time. Until then, he and Eddie studied the maps of the spice-producing countries and made frequent journeys to London to visit the spice merchants at Eastcheap. Although the Food and Drugs Act of 1860 had meant that the adulteration of foods and spices was a rare occurrence, they made their purchases with great care. Prior to that Act, it was not uncommon to find meat and fish products coloured with red lead, bottled fruits containing copper, and curry powder and cayenne contaminated with mercury. Some alcoholic drinks had been enlivened with tincture of capsicum or essence of cayenne, products more likely to increase the effect of a hangover than produce a refreshing beverage.

It is not surprising, therefore, that food products bore labels testifying to their purity and wholesomeness. Doctor Alfred Bostock Hill, public analyst and Birmingham's first Medical Officer of Health, had tested all the products made by the Midland Vinegar Company. They had won his complete approval. Not so another company's vinegar, which had produced the following comment 'Warranted to riddle the coat of any stomach, even that of an ostrich'. If the new Sauce were to succeed, it was clear that Doctor Hill's good opinion would be vital.

In 1901 the Moores registered the offices of F.G. Garton's Sauce Manufactory at Tower Road, Aston Manor, but still the moment was not auspicious for the launching of the Sauce. The old queen had died, the nation was in mourning and HP Sauce must wait in the wings a little longer. Meanwhile Samson purchased the unsuccessful Vulcan Brewery, opposite his premises, for use as a bottling department.

By 1903 the excitement of a new century was in the air. Victoria, although deeply respected, had never been the merriest of monarchs, but her son had a distinct air of bonhomie. The telephone had been invented, the houses of the rich were lit by electricity, important messages could be sent by wireless telegraphy, the horseless carriage had appeared, and men had taken a few shaky flights in the aeroplane. The desire for novelty was everywhere and Samson was ready to satisfy it. Thousands of green glass bottles were displayed in food stores great and small. Their labels, decorated with a tasteful illustration of the Houses of Parliament, all bore the following opinion of A. Bostock Hill, MD, FIC: 'I have analysed the sample of Garton's HP Sauce and find it to be made from the best materials. The well-known Midland Vinegar Company's vinegar, than which in my opinion there is no better, is used in its preparation. It is of a pleasant and piquant flavour and is in every respect a THOROUGHLY GOOD SAUCE'.

Would the public agree with his verdict?

Menu

SOUP.

FISH.

ENTREES.

JOINTS.

VEGETABLES.

SWEETS.

MAKE A POINT OF TRYING H.P. SAUCE YOU WILL FIND IT ON EACH OF THE TABLES.

The first quarter century, during which HP goes to the Front and we say goodbye to an old friend

The public's verdict on the new Sauce was as favourable as Samson could ever have hoped. The Midland Vinegar Company, as well as producing its well-known vinegar and pickles, was now struggling to meet the demand for its new product. It was forced into the happy position of having to acquire yet more land on which to build stables, carpenters' shops, blacksmiths' forges and stores for the increasing number of casks of maturing vinegar.

But Samson was too shrewd to become complacent about his success. The initial impact of HP Sauce must be followed by an advertising campaign to outdo any that had gone before. His imagination fired, he explained his idea to Eddie and his other business associates with great enthusiasm. A fleet of small, covered wagons was to be assembled, which would travel the country piled high with miniature bottles of HP Sauce. His audience approved, although venturing to suggest that the plan was perhaps just a little unexciting. Samson paused dramatically before delivering his *coup de grâce*. These wagons, he then pro-claimed, were to be drawn by ZEBRAS! His listeners could not believe their ears. Zebras were known to be impossible to train, and they had visions of these creatures bucking and bolting in the streets while miniature bottles of HP rolled and smashed in

The launching of HP Sauce

the gutters. Samson was eventually persuaded that donkeys might be a more practicable idea.

The impact of these appealing little animals was enormous, and the campaign a resounding success. The miniature bottles of Sauce remained safely intact, for, as anyone who has any dealings with donkeys has discovered, these animals, amenable to no sort of persuasion, choose their own pace, which is invariably slow. This campaign was followed a few years later by another, whereby any housewife producing a bottle of HP Sauce on demand would receive 10*s*. (a not inconsiderable sum at a time when a basic weekly wage could be 7*s*.6*d*. and the average take-home pay of a man working at the Midland Vinegar Company was around 15*s*. a week).

But if imaginative advertising was one factor that persuaded the nation to buy HP Sauce, a glance at contemporary eating habits provides another. We possess a recipe book compiled by Jennifer's grandmother at the beginning of the century for the education of her young and inexperienced cook. In this, the recipes for puddings are many and substantial. Bearing such names as Black Cap Pudding, Russian Pudding, Spanish Cream, A Good Trifle, Fun Pudding and Patriotic Pudding (a white mould covered with raspberry jam but mercifully with no hint of blue), they contain quantities of cream and eggs that would shock today's nutritionists. Alcohol, for instance brandy or sherry, is a frequent addition and most contain the warmer spices, that is, nutmeg, ginger and cinnamon.

The meat and fish dishes contain no added flavouring apart from the obligatory salt and pepper and an infrequent pinch of mixed herbs or nutmeg. However, the ingredients for chutneys and pickles contain large amounts of garlic, cayenne and mustard seed, while in a recipe for a tomato chutney a dozen red chillies are required. Hot stuff indeed! The British taste for spices, absent in the cooking of their meat and fish dishes, surfaced in the chutneys and sauces that were served with them at table. HP now joined their number. (Let it not be imagined that in households of any social pretension the HP bottle ever appeared on the table. The contents would be poured into a fine china or cut-glass dish before the meal and this would be placed on the table accompanied by a small spoon. This custom continued for several decades.)

Britain was not the only nation to develop a taste for HP Sauce, our colonies quickly became addicted. It was introduced originally by the firm's travellers, sailing abroad with cases packed with samples and illustrated price lists, which boasted that these products were of 'intimately British appeal'. That the life of these intrepid travellers was hardly luxurious is illustrated by the following itinerary of one E.L. Cooke.

1902   Dec 1: Sailed for Cape Town on S.S. *Scott*.
        Dec 23: Arrived Table Bay. No salary, only
        expenses.
1903   Aug 6: Left South Africa for Australia per
        S.S. *Runic*.
        Sep 4: Arrived Sydney £3 15s.0d. plus 50 per
        cent commission.
1904   May 13: Left Australia for South Africa per
        S.S. *Suevic*.
        June 14: Arrive Table Bay. £5. No
        commission, half pay on water.
        Oct 5: Arrive Southampton.
1905   Canada: £4 10s.0d. No commission, no half pay.
1905   Home: £3 15s.0d. per week. No commission.

Mr Cooke's long sea voyages were seemingly unrelieved by riotous living!

Soon, thanks to such intrepid travellers and the growing reputation of HP Sauce, it became the practice for merchants in foreign countries to apply for the agency to distribute it themselves. New Zealand was the first customer, soon followed by Canada. Indeed, the demand from Canada was such that a chart was kept at Aston showing the times at which the St. Lawrence River would be free of ice. Deliveries could thus be arranged so that disappointment would be avoided. Sweden and Denmark were keen customers also, finding that HP Sauce much enlivened the ubiquitous Scandinavian meatball. The United States of America was purchasing the Sauce by 1913, and South Africa a few years later.

Ironically, in view of the image it later acquired as the common man's sauce, HP was considered quite a luxury in Britain at that time. But although its price of 6*d*. for a large bottle was no small sum for the working man, its popularity flourished unabated. Continuing to prosper, the Moores expanded their business with the manufacture of other products and made plans for a yeast factory. Modernisation also continued with the purchase of the first lorry in 1912, followed by that of several motor vans and in 1913 motor cycles were provided for the sales representatives. (Several of these gentlemen were seen to make distinctly shaky exits from the factory on this novel form of transport!)

Although HP Sauce was now an established favourite, it was still kept in the public eye by advertisements declaring it to be 'the sauce that never cloys' and that 'no well regulated home should be without it'. One well-known hoarding poster portrayed a small dejected mongrel gazing up at his master, who has obviously just finished every morsel of a large meal, made even tastier by HP. The caption reads 'The Poor Little Dog had None'. Another famous but, to our mind, rather sad caption read 'Mary had a Little Lamb with lots of HP Sauce'. Painting and hand-writing competitions were promoted for children, offering solid gold medals as prizes. Delightful books, their verses based on popular nursery rhymes, were produced. The following is a sample.

Georgy Porgy pudding and pie
Kissed the girls and made them cry
At once his mother hurried out
And said 'What's all the noise about?
I've often told you, naughty boy
That little girls you mayn't annoy
And since you will not let them play
You'll have no HP Sauce today.'
This punishment proved so severe,
That Georgy now is quite a dear.

In the February, 1913 edition of *Home Notes*, a well-known magazine for women, another advertisement for HP appears. This depicts a distraught young wife holding an empty Sauce bottle, with the caption 'None Left: what *will* he say?' In the same edition, an article entitled 'Costumes for Easter' states 'Excepting for the introduction of side pleats, there are as yet few changes in fashion'. But if there were few changes in the world of fashion, there were to be dramatic changes in the world at large. In June 1914 Archduke Franz Ferdinand was assassinated at Sarajevo. A few months later Jennifer's grandmother patriotically crossed out the entry for 'German Sausage' in her recipe book. On 4 September the Great War had begun.

None left !
what will he say?

—and he enjoys H.P. Sauce so much because it tempts the appetite.

If you only knew the delicious flavour of this much-talked-of Sauce you would know why it is so welcome at every meal — every day.

Wouldn't it be worth your while to try a bottle of the one and only

H.P.
SAUCE

Grocers sell H.P. Sauce in large **6**d. *bottles.*

The Midland Vinegar Co., Ltd., Birmingham.

Sing a song of sixpence
A pocket full of rye
Four and twenty blackbirds
Baked in a pie

When the pie was open
The birds began to sing~
"A little **H·P Sauce** would make
This pie fit for a King"

The male workforce at HP began to leave in ever-increasing numbers to fight for their country. Faced with heavy demands from the government for supplies of vinegar and sauce for the troops, the Moores were now obliged to relax one of their rules. Previously Samson had refused to employ married women, firmly believing that 'a woman's place was in the home'. Wives and mothers now came to swell the depleted workforce at 'The Sauce'! They worked hard to do their bit for the country, and any ideas Samson might have had about a 'weaker sex' must have been quickly dispersed. Small female figures were in complete control of the huge workhorses beside which they appeared so tiny. Other

Lilian A Govey

women, rolling back their sleeves with determination, managed to roll large casks of vinegar onto the drays.

These women who worked so hard, also had their small compensatory pleasures. At that time there was no official tea break and woe betide anyone caught with a cup in their hand. The men may have complied with this rule, but not so their womenfolk. Bottles of tea, made at home, were smuggled into work and surreptitiously reheated on steam pipes or in buckets of boiling water. The management may well have had a suspicion of such practices, but the prospect of facing a crowd of women who have been deprived of their 'cuppa' was such a daunting one that they wisely turned their heads the other way.

Large supplies of HP Sauce were sent to the troops throughout the war. Many men claimed it was the only thing that made an unvarying diet of bully beef palatable. In 1917 Samson introduced an innovation, of great consequence to the future linguistic education of British children. On the label for the first time there now appeared the famous paragraph extolling the virtues of HP Sauce, written in French. The first version of this French text to be produced was discovered to carry undertones of a rather suggestive nature. Red-faced with embarrassment, those responsible quickly produced a second and innocuous version — 'Absolument pure', as the label states of the Sauce. The text ran thus:

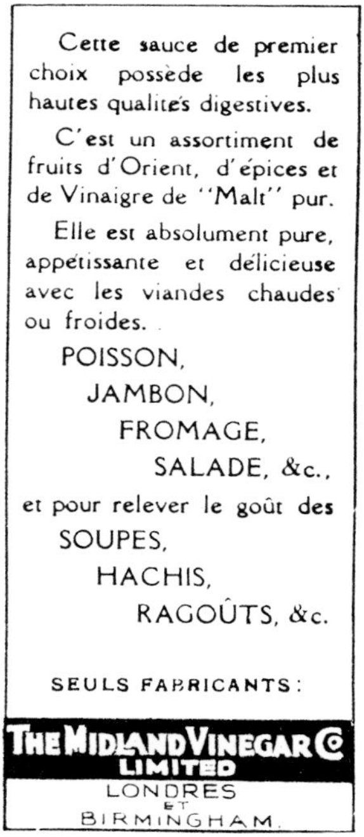

Cette sauce de premier choix possède les plus hautes qualités digestives.

C'est un assortiment de fruits d'Orient, d'épices et de Vinaigre de ''Malt'' pur.

Elle est absolument pure, appétissante et délicieuse avec les viandes chaudes ou froides.

POISSON,

JAMBON,

FROMAGE,

SALADE, &c.,

et pour relever le goût des

SOUPES,

HACHIS,

RAGOÛTS, &c.

SEULS FABRICANTS:

THE MIDLAND VINEGAR C⁰
LIMITED
LONDRES
ET
BIRMINGHAM.

It has been popularly assumed that this new addition to the HP label was either a tribute to our allies in the First World War or a recognition of the huge quantities of the Sauce consumed by British troops in France. In fact, it was a definite attempt to, in modern parlance, 'Upmarket' the product. As the menu for any sophisticated dinner was always written in French, it was hoped the new label would help to associate HP Sauce with the glories of French cuisine.

Whether this rather bold attempt succeeded or not is uncertain, but the fact remains that these words were the first in any foreign language to be read and learnt by millions of British children. The wording has varied over the years. Dinsdale distinctly remembers a version beginning with the words 'Cette sauce de premier choix'. Jennifer has recollections of one commencing 'Cette sauce de haute qualité', which proves, she adds, Dinsdale's considerable seniority!

On 11 November 1918 the Armistice was signed, and 'the war to end all wars' was over. Nearly three-quarters of a million people had perished. Now the survivors, many irreparably damaged, straggled home. Apart from family reunions, the prospect facing them was a bleak one. Much bitterness was aroused by the lack of decent housing and the extensive unemployment with which they were greeted.

Those returning to HP were luckier. Their wives and girlfriends had kept their jobs warm for them and now moved out, so that the men could regain their old employment. The married women returned to their domestic hearth, and single girls only continued to be the rule at 'The Sauce' until the Second World War. (Meanwhile they had won their own battle over the tea break and from now on a tea trolley trundled around the factory twice a day.)

Business boomed for the Moores in the immediate post-war years. A splendid sports ground was built for the workforce and the practice of a week's holiday with pay was established. But although, as keen as ever, he visited the factory every morning, with an eye for anything untoward, Samson was an ageing man. In 1921 he retired and in 1924 the Midland Vinegar Company was sold to the British Share Holders Trust, which floated it as a public company under the name HP Sauce Ltd. 'Eddie' Moore also retired, while his sons preferred pursuing university careers to working in the family business. Thus the Moores disappear from subsequent chapters of the HP story.

Samson Moore died at the age of seventy-seven. His energy, ambition and acute business sense had resulted in a success very typical of his time. His high moral tone was balanced by a great love of life. There was a touch of the dandy in his daily button-hole of a fresh carnation and more than a hint of Barnum and Bailey about some of his schemes for advertising. He developed a great fondness for oysters during the latter part of his life and, having purchased a country estate, threw himself into the role of country squire with gusto.

His son 'Eddie' had qualities that complemented those of his more extrovert and expansive father. Innovative and highly conscientious, he paid great attention to detail. Indeed his insistence on testing the quality of each fresh batch of HP Sauce at his own dinner table exasperated his wife greatly and led to its banishment to the kitchen. It is a gentle face that looks at us from his photograph, enlivened by a twinkle in the eye.

Together, father and son made a formidable partnership, which provided employment for several generations of families in Aston Manor. They also bequeathed a legacy, in the contents of a bottle, to be found in the store cupboards of the world. How would their heirs, HP Sauce Ltd, deal with this precious in-heritance?

'Eddie' Moore

The 1920s and 1930s:
the 'One and Only' triumphs through
times of trouble and strife

By 1925 HP Sauce Ltd was a public company, its only connection
with Samson Moore being the appointment of a son-in-law as
managing director. The new management, however, wisely continued to run the company on similar lines to their predecessors
and maintained the atmosphere of a family business. The local
workforce had now been augmented by the more exotic figures
of university graduates, employed in managerial posts or as
chemists in the rapidly expanding laboratory. The latter were
regarded with deepest suspicion by some of the older hands,
whose ideas of a laboratory owed much to the tale of Frankens-
tein. There was still plenty of work for the massive but gentle
dray horses, but an increasing number of motor vans and lor-
ries were to be seen, their sides emblazoned with the proud and
irrefutable slogan 'The One and Only HP Sauce'.

   Amidst the scenes of increasing mechanisation one factor
remained constant. The unique odour that emanated from the
Sauce factory. A gentleman who passed his childhood in Aston
during the Twenties describes it now, with considerable tact, as
'a heady aroma'. A more affectionate description came from a
lady now living in the Home Counties. 'Warm, yeasty and com-
forting', was how she put it, adding with a sigh, 'There's

Painting book 1922

nothing like it in Chalfont St Giles!' Local teachers when chiding their pupils for lateness or absenteeism were often met with the retort, 'Please miss it was the smell from "The Sauce", it made me feel sick'. An explanation received with suspicion tinged with sympathy.

The world outside the gates of the HP factory was an exciting place for some in these first few years of peace. Cinemas were being built all over the country and Aston now boasted its own Globe Electric Theatre, enthusiastically patronised by the HP workforce. Women now had the vote (a fact that would have given Samson Moore no great satisfaction) and celebrated their new status by shortening their skirts and bobbing their hair. (Photos of the time show that calves developed on the hockey fields of England were unwisely revealed by the shorter skirts.) The privileged youth of the Jazz Age kicked up their heels to the music of the Charleston, began a vogue for cocktails, and smoked their cigarettes, women included, through holders of incredible length. But if for some, like Barbara Cartland, the Twenties were a time spent 'Charlestoning the night away' for others they were years of poverty and frustration.

The men who had returned from the horrors of the trenches

had not found Britain a 'land fit for heroes to live in' as promised. Jobs were hard to come by and the dole was insufficient to support families as yet not limited by contraception. In times of danger or depression, the retention of small luxuries becomes of great importance. HP has always sold well in times of financial hardship, and now was no exception. The Sauce was an expensive item on the shopping list of the poor but many a family managed to have a precious bottle on their table. Many children of that time including the dignified head waiter of our favourite restaurant now recall their main meal of the day consisting of two slices of bread with a careful scraping of HP Sauce sandwiched between.

Industrial unrest was evident and on the increase. Provoked by the appalling cuts in wages and employment proposed for coal miners, the TUC declared a General Strike on 3 May 1926. For many of the citizens of Birmingham, the nine days that followed brought no great inconvenience into their lives. Petrol was plentiful, stocks of food in the shops were high and the Cooperative movement helped the families of strikers. Some violence did occur on picket lines and an inevitable degree of tension between the police force and the strikers gradually developed. These incidents apart, law and order were maintained and the only troops seen were those making a ceremonial appearance at a local tattoo. On HP Sauce, the effect of the strike, as on many family-type businesses, was minimal, although union membership increased.

By 12 May the General Strike was over, but its aftermath was not a happy one. Many employers refused to reinstate workers who had been most actively involved in the strike. These men joined the already alarming numbers of unemployed and the bleak economic outlook was worsened by news from America of the Wall Street crash in 1929.

HP was doing its best to provide some welcome relief during these cheerless times. New bottling and labelling machines were introduced, the speed of which at first filled their girl operatives with pure terror, but enabled the Sauce to be supplied at an even faster rate to an eager public. When a piece of pie filled with the meat off a pig's backbone, which could be purchased for 3d., or a dish of potato cakes was considered a luxury by many, it was no wonder that a spot of 'the sauce that never cloys' was a welcome addition.

The company expanded to produce further titillations for the jaded palate by making a tomato ketchup and a salad cream. From the outset, Samson Moore had believed that HP Sauce would hold the greatest appeal for the working and lower middle classes, and his advertisement campaigns had been largely slanted in their direction. That this policy was still continuing is shown by a report compiled in 1931 by Mather and Crowther, the company's advertising agents. This suggests that 'Trade in the London area has perhaps suffered a little by... appealing to the working classes more than to the better type of user, who has taste and discrimination'.

Whether or not as a result of this, HP certainly had not the snob appeal of Lea and Perrins Worcestershire sauce. Made to the recipe of a noble lord and favoured by the food-loving French, it was felt to have a certain social cachet. It was therefore something of a triumph for the humbler condiment when in the early 1930s HP Sauce Ltd acquired Lea and Perrins Ltd by an exchange of shares.

The advertising campaigns reflect the tastes and conditions of the times. At the beginning of the 1930s the depressed state of industry produced great stress of economy. One advertisement patriotically paraphrased 'Today England expects every man and woman to be economical', and then urged 'Use HP Sauce and make the most of every scrap of fish or meat or cheese.'

It's the taste that saves the waste— **H.P.** SAUCE ensures that *everything* is "eaten up" with utmost enjoyment.

A national competition produced this winning slogan, 'It's the taste that saves the waste', coupled with the assurance that 'such deliciousness as you get only with HP Sauce ensures that EVERYTHING is eaten up with utmost enjoyment'. 'HP Sauce makes frugal fare regal' must surely have given encouragement to housewives struggling to make ends meet. Those lucky enough to be able to afford a weekly joint of meat were encouraged to use every morsel. They were advised that HP was 'The Sauce that's Right for meat that's Left', encouraged to add 'A dash to the hash' and assured that 'made-up dishes, the bugbear of every cook will present no more problems if HP Sauce is used'.

Then, as now, the health-giving virtues of all products were emphasised and vitamins were declared to be present in everything from custard to nail polish. The health-enhancing properties of HP Sauce, too, were underlined. Stress was laid on the purity of the ingredients, and the lack of artificial preservatives, and much was made of its properties as a digestive relish. 'Don't just peck at food — tackle it with real hearty gusto. That's the way to keep fit' read the small print of one advertisement. Accompanying these words was the picture of a disgustingly healthy looking chap tucking into a plateful of bacon and eggs. Surrounding him was the caption 'Give your appetite a tonic. HP Sauce with EVERY meal'.

This particular advertisement made an indelible impression on one small girl according to a newspaper report. Noticing one day that her pet goldfish appeared a trifle listless she proceeded to fetch a bottle of HP and pour its contents into their bowl.

Sometime later her mother, noticing the rather murky quality of the water, promptly drained and refilled the bowl. It may say

"*Look Mummy*

that's where they make the **H.P. Sauce**"

A child actually made this remark when passing the Houses of Parliament. Though her Mother laughingly corrected her, the child would not be convinced, but ran up to a policeman and said: "Please, Mr. Policeman, they do make H.P. Sauce here — don't they?"

Of course, the little lady — only seven years old — recognised the building from the view on every bottle of H.P. Sauce, a very familiar sight in her home. If she had read the recent advertisements in this paper, or built up the model of the Houses of Parliament given away at Christmas she would have known that H.P. Sauce is only *named* after the Houses of Parliament.

HP *Large bottle* 9ᴰ
Picnic size 3ᴰ

SAUCE

something for the quality of the sauce that the fish survived this misadventure with no ill effects.

In spite of the fairly recent emancipation of women and the increasing numbers of them employed in jobs and professional careers, the women in the HP advertisements seem an old-fashioned lot. Neat and respectable with genteelly pretty features, their brows are faintly furrowed by the responsibility of pleasing their menfolk. 'What will my husband say to me? Here's more cold meat and no HP' wails one typical example. 'The Dainty for Dinner' and 'For Daintier Meals — HP Sauce' were slogans aimed at a proportion of the female population presumed to be

Make the Cold Shoulder Welcome

Whether you do, or do not, know the origin of the "Cold Shoulder," last minute guests are easily catered for—where there's H.P. Sauce in the cupboard. The remains of joints (mutton, beef or pork), sandwiches, corned beef, meat pasties—all taste delicious with the rich, piquant fruity flavour of H.P. to help them along. Of course, you always use H.P. Sauce with bacon, cheese, roasts and grills. It's just as good for 'made-up' dishes such as rissoles, hashes, fish cakes, or Shepherd's Pie.

Cold Joints go better with

H P SAUCE

9ᵈ a bottle.
Picnic size 3d.

Simply grand with Sardines for Tea!

much concerned with such 'period' refinements as paper doilies, tiered cake stands and pastry forks. However, another slogan 'Why cook so often? Serve it cold with HP' suggests that an increasing number of women were no longer so willing to slave over a hot stove at the end of a hard day's work at office or factory.

When we look at the menus of the Thirties, the continuing popularity of HP is no surprise. To modern-day tastes, they seem colourless and unimaginative and in need of some extra zest.

Salt, pepper, cheese and onion were the usual savoury flavourings, and parsley and, to a much lesser extent, mint were the only herbs used in any quantity. White sauces, flavoured with nothing more than salt and pepper, smothered a multitude of culinary boredom. *Woman's Own*, in an edition of 1932, advised the ideal contents of a store cupboard for the price of]1 3*s*.5½*d*. Tucked away amongst large amounts of flour, macaroni, sago and rice is one small packet of mixed herbs.

Foreign cuisine was restricted to the restaurants of the big cities, or to a few houses of the wealthy and cosmopolitan. Tentative attempts *were* made to introduce it to a wider British public and the foreword to a collection of international recipes published at the time began 'It is a mistake to think that foreign cookery is "messy"!' The British remained largely unmoved, however, and HP was having none of it. 'New elaborate recipes are published almost daily but experienced housewives know that simple homely fare is best and nothing satisfies or pleases more than old-fashioned dishes' ran the words of one of their advertisements.

And what were these dishes thus heartily endorsed? Boiled Mutton, Cottage Pie, Hot Pot, Rissoles, Herrings, Boiled White Fish were all recommended, as were cold meats served with that peculiarly British salad of lettuce, tomato, cucumber, hard-boiled egg and boiled beetroot. HP Sauce or salad cream might accompany the latter, but never a wicked French dressing. While the quality and freshness of the ingredients used at that time were often superior to those of today, it comes as no surprise to find the British love of spices evident in the pickles and bottled sauces they used with such food.

HP's popularity abroad was also growing. By the end of the decade, agencies had been established in over thirty different countries. Many of these, as is to be expected, were British colonies, but glancing through the files of that time one notices the exotic names of Shanghai, Estonia and Latvia. The last entry in the Chinese file dated 1937 reads ominously, 'Trade conditions rendered difficult by reason of Sino-Japanese conflict'.

In Europe too, conflict seemed inevitable to some people. By 1939 Hitler's desire for world domination led to his invasion of Poland and on 3 September in that year Chamberlain had the dreadful task of telling the British people that, once again, their country was at war with Germany. The nation braced itself for the fight ahead and HP prepared to make its own particular contribution to the war effort.

Make your Food Budget go Further with

H P SAUCE

H.P. Sauce will help you to use up every scrap of meat, fish, vegetables, etc. H.P. improves all roasts and grills, savouries and made-up dishes. Here is one excellent recipe :—

BAKED EGG BELFORT

Cut the tops of some large tomatoes and scoop out insides. Half fill with chopped cold meat mixed with a teaspoonful of H.P. Sauce. Add tiny piece of butter or margarine. Break an egg into each. Stand on greased tin and bake in moderate oven.

Wise house-wives know the value of H.P. Sauce in wartime. Buy a bottle to-day.

HP joins the fight

During the first few weeks following the declaration of war the British public prepared for invasion. Sandbags were filled, windows were taped or covered by wooden shutters at night-time as prevention against shattered glass and blackout curtains were hung to prevent any chink of light giving assistance to enemy bombers. The government issued an ABC of air-raid precaution in which, among much technical information, was advice of a cosier nature: 'Eat good meals during the strain' was one such precept. 'Go to bed earlier and rise at an earlier hour these blackout days' was perhaps a less inviting idea to some. Suggestions were made as to the best way of passing the time spent in air-raid shelters: 'Jars, screwtops, should be kept filled with barley sugar and raisins to nibble during a raid'. While those good with their hands might 'knit blankets, bed socks, mufflers, etc. from odd pieces of wool, or unwound wool, which will unravel if washed in soapy water or tightly wound round a hot water bottle'. For those of a literary bent the advice was: 'Read something light ... try E.M. Delderfield, P.G. Wodehouse or Beverley Nichols' garden books'!

Many children from the large industrial cities were evacuated to country areas for their safety. The evacuation area of Birmingham included Aston, so, with young men being conscripted, many of the HP employees found their families sadly depleted. Eventually only the highly skilled technicians at HP were excused from being called up. Once more married women stepped into the breach and returned to the Sauce factory, where for their safety a basement had been converted into an air-raid shelter.

The first few months of war proved uneventful and the population became less apprehensive. By the end of the year, Winston Churchill had succeeded as Prime Minister, the devastating Blitz of London had begun and Birmingham, too, had suffered its first bombs. By the end of the following year, after the bombing of Pearl Harbor, America had joined the fight against both Hitler and Japan. The war continued, seemingly endless, with its privations and the heart-rending death toll of civilians and armed forces alike.

But by 1944 the tide began to turn in the allies' favour and in August Paris was liberated. At the beginning of 1945 the first boat train since 1940 left London for France. On 7 May the Germans unconditionally surrendered. The exhausted British people now longed for a peaceful family life and no more blood, sweat and tears. In the next General Election, a Labour government was swept to power.

During the years of war HP had not neglected its duty. The workforce had become fire fighters, air-raid wardens, formed their own Home Guard company, driven ambulances and learnt First Aid. Their biggest responsibility had been to cope with the demand for the Sauce from both the armed forces and the civilian population. The uncertain availability of raw materials and the priority of supplying the troops meant that HP was often hard to find in certain parts of the country.

A lady living in Devon recalls the wartime visit of her brother and his family, who were seeking a brief respite from the bombings of their home town, Exeter. They all, her brother especially, seemed rather jaded, and their kind hostess worked hard to provide the best meals she could produce at a time of acute food shortages. A talented cook, she was justifiably proud of the results of her labours and yet an air of gloom still hung about her brother's countenance. A little upset at this reaction to her skills, she questioned her sister-in-law as to the reason. This lady hastily assured her of the excellence of the cuisine, but nervously confessed that her husband was that not uncommon creature, an HP addict. The Sauce had been unavailable recently and he was missing his 'fix'.

The beauties of the Devon countryside were forgotten for the remainder of the holiday as lengthy forays were made to village shops and distant market towns. Eventually, exhausted, but triumphantly bearing a modest supply of the vital bottles, the brother returned to Exeter a happier man.

But if the British were dismayed at the scarcity of HP Sauce, so too were their Canadian cousins as supplies had dwindled owing to the hazards of transatlantic shipping. Luckily a happy solution was found. A most amiable relationship had been established with the well-known firm of E.D. Smith of Ontario, which had supplied HP for many years with tomato purée, and it was decided to licence them to make the Sauce in Canada. It was a momentous decision as, since the days of Samson Moore, the recipe had been a closely guarded secret. A positively cloak and dagger operation was set in motion. The recipe was translated into code and sent in two separate halves across the Atlantic, with the method and description of the plant following later in a third envelope.

While the Canadians could now blithely pour HP over their enviable steaks, it was a different story in Britain. Every precious drop of the bottle was used with care in order to conserve enough to add zest to meagre meals until another bottle was available. Food rationing had commenced, in early 1940, the first victims being bacon, butter and sugar. 'Make your Food Budget go further with HP Sauce' was the immediate response of the advertisements. 'No coupons needed' was the claim of a recipe for 'Ham Macaroni' recommended as a (rather heavy) breakfast dish and strongly flavoured with HP Sauce.

Porchester Pie, with beef sausages as the main ingredient, was another recipe recommended by HP. Sausages were but pale imitations now of their pre-war selves. Largely composed of breadcrumbs, their main virtue lay in the fact that they were unrationed. A small economy label with the Ministry of Food insignia now appeared on HP bottles and the attractive Garton's label disappeared for ever. Advertising for the Sauce gradually ceased.

Since demand far exceeded supply, it would have been uncharitable to rub salt into the wounds of the deprived. But if the advertisements had stopped, not so the search both for HP and for ways of augmenting rationed foods.

The population was encouraged to 'Dig for Victory' and allotments of land were eagerly sought after. Proud herbaceous borders disappeared to be replaced by beds of turnips. Pig rearing soared in popularity, although only half of the eventual carcass could be retained by the owner of the animal. That these efforts were worthwhile is shown by the following list of foods allowed each person in 1944.

Bacon and ham	—	4 oz per week
Tea	—	2 oz per week
Meat	—	1s.2d. worth per week
Cheese	—	2 oz per week
Butter	—	2 oz per week
Shell eggs	—	1 egg per 2 weeks
Dried eggs	—	1 packet per 4 weeks
Liquid milk	—	2½ pints per week

Great ingenuity was used with HP Sauce. One farmer's wife added a bottle of Sauce to her own plum jam to produce an 'instant' chutney. Because of the importance of their work, coal miners were allowed a cheese ration larger than the national average, and their wives combined HP Sauce and cheese in many different ways.

The meals of the population generally were of limited variety and often scanty proportion. The food of that time has become inextricably associated with the infamous 'Woolton' Pie! From a recipe issued by Lord Woolton, Minister of Food, it consisted of pastry topping a selection of root vegetables, carrots, swedes, turnips, even maybe mangle wurzels! It hardly comes as a surprise, therefore, to learn that HP was more popular than ever.

The armed forces were no less grateful than the civilian population for their supplies of HP Sauce. It not only rendered food more palatable, but for some provided a welcome reminder of life back home. One ex-employee of the Sauce factory, serving in the Royal Navy, found himself in Iceland at one stage of the war. His surroundings proving less than congenial, he began to

suffer severe attacks of homesickness. However, help was at hand
in the shape of a small shop in Reykjavik, which stocked HP
Sauce. The young sailor would spend hours gazing at the familiar
bottles in the shop window and come away feeling much com-
forted. 'It was better than a seat at the flicks', he later declared.

Other members of the HP workforce who served in the armed
forces recall with gratitude the food parcels they received from
'The Sauce' during the war. One gentleman, who later rose to
the dizziest heights of managerial responsibility but was at the
time a junior clerk in the purchasing department, was sent for
his initial RAF training to the salubrious resort of Blackpool. He
found himself billeted in one of the town's many boarding houses.
Alas, his landlady, due to the exigencies of war, was unable to
provide the quality of meals she had been used to serving the
bucket and spade brigade. Hearing of this sad plight, the factory at Aston rushed to the young man's rescue. Arriving back
at his billet one day he was astounded to find every spare inch
of the entrance hall occupied by crates containing three gross
bottles of HP Sauce. Being a man of principle, he resisted the
temptation to make a financial profit out of his windfall, but
generous gifts of the precious bottles won him lasting popularity
in the area.

For some, the aroma emanating from the factory when HP
Sauce is brewing has never held any attraction. But, indirectly,
it proved of much value to a member of the RAF in an unpleasant
situation. His story is an intriguing one. In pre-war days he had

lived in Aston, next door to a family with two young daughters. The younger of the two had needed regular outpatient treatment at an orthopaedic hospital in Birmingham, and elder sister Peggy always accompanied her on these visits. The pair would board the No.2 tram, but by the time they reached Aston Station the younger girl would inevitably have become distinctly green around the gills and complain of feeling sick. 'It's the smell of the Sauce', she would wail and the sisters would be forced to disembark. A restorative walk around Woolworths would then be necessary before the afflicted girl felt well enough to continue the journey.

Peggy became distinctly weary of this routine. Her younger sister was never actually sick, the journey took twice as long, and, to add insult to injury, by breaking their journey they had to pay an extra $1d.$ to get to their destination. However, she had heard that brown paper was a certain cure for travel sickness, although in what form was unclear. Being a resourceful girl, she purchased a large sheet of said paper, and immediately prior to their next outing cut a large hole in it and placed it over her sister's head. Wearing this improvised tabard, the younger girl was able to reach Birmingham without any break in the journey or feelings of nausea. Everyone was most impressed and details of the cure were given to the next door neighbours, whose son Ron also suffered from travel sickness.

The years passed, Peggy grew up and became a teacher and when war was declared Ron enlisted in the RAF. Some twenty years later, the pair met again at a party. They had begun reminiscing about old times, when Ron suddenly expressed his deep gratitude to her for the 'brown paper cure' for travel sickness. It had proved completely successful in his case and he had special reason to be thankful for that. During the war his plane had been shot down over the sea. He had then, with other of the plane's crew, spent several days in a small life raft on a far from calm ocean and he had been the only man never to have become sea-sick.

And so, in ways expected and unexpected, HP Sauce had given some small help to the nation at war. Now in 1945, peace had returned, but times were still far from easy and its presence on the British table would be as welcome as ever.

Post-war years and
the 1950s

Bonfires had blazed from hilltops throughout the land and people
had danced in the streets when the end of the war was declared,
but the immediate post-war years were times of greyness and
austerity, with the nation struggling to repair the damaged fabric
of its personal and commercial lives. A women's magazine advised
the would-be hostess of the late 1940s that 'the main course
should not include meat as most people feel embarrassed if they
are offered other people's rations'. The weather decided to make
its own unique contribution to these cheerless times and the winter
of 1946 + 7 proved to be one of the worst on record.

But colour and change returned slowly to the nation's life.
On 20 November 1947, the greyness of London was dispelled
by the bright colours of myriad military uniforms and the sounds
of horses' hooves and rattling sabres filled the air. This was no
martial occasion but a joyful day as a future Queen of England
was escorted to her wedding by the Household Cavalry. A nation
starved of colour and ceremony roared its approval. By the end
of the 1940s, although food was still rationed and fuel in short
supply, the rationing of petrol and clothes had ended. How had
HP fared during these first post-war years?

The demand for the piquant Sauce during this time of austerity was greater than ever, and the company had plans to expand their premises and increase production. However building restrictions applied to the manufacturers of the country's most famous Sauce as much as to everyone else. Instead they fulfilled their responsibility to the nation's palate by purchasing the old established firms of Macks of Walsall and Fletchers of Selby, renowned respectively for pickles and sauces.

Members of the workforce, demobbed from the services, were delighted to be working at 'The Sauce' again. But there was an important difference between the current situation and that pertaining at the end of the First World War. Then the married women, who had worked so valiantly throughout the war, had been obliged to vacate their jobs. Now, if they so wished, they could remain. It had taken two world wars and much hard labour to remove the prohibition caused by Samson Moore's disapproval. (Delighted as women were to work at 'The Sauce', they still had a grumble. Many of them swore that the smell produced by the brewing of HP Sauce so stimulated their appetites that they found themselves gaining up to a stone in weight.')

Private cars began to reappear on the firm's premises, while another form of transport made its final exit. In the 1930s HP had still owned nearly forty dray horses. In 1948, Billy, the last of these gentle giants, pulled his final cartload of empty barrels and was honourably retired to green pastures.

The economy label on the Sauce bottles also disappeared, to be replaced by labelling less decorative than the pre-war version, but with its French paragraph still intact. The shape of the bottles themselves had been slightly modified and these were now supplied by the Albion Bottle Co. of Oldbury, in which firm HP had now acquired shares.

And so, gradually improving and modernising its equipment, HP Sauce Ltd prepared to move into the second half of the twentieth century. Advertising began to appear in a more lavish form and great stress was laid on the maintenance of pre-war quality. Food was still rationed and recipes issued by the Ministry of Food bore such headings as 'Dishes for hot summer days that don't eat into the meat ration'. But the Fifties were to see an accelerated rise in the standard of living. It was also to be the last decade where that tradition of eating, of which HP was an

1952: 'The Sauce' celebrates the Coronation

integral part, would remain pre-eminent.

The beginning of the Fifties seemed little changed from the latter half of the Forties. Articles in women's magazines still bore depressingly familiar headings, such as 'Limited rations but unlimited imagination'. But foods unseen for years were gradually reappearing in the shops, and many children now sampled their first bananas.

National Service was still compulsory and was to remain so for several more years. For some young men this was a time of broadening horizons, for many others it was a frustrating period spent in the performance of irksome ritual and apparently worthless jobs. But for all of them, it offered new experiences, if sometimes of an unexpected kind. For Dinsdale, raised in a respectable South Coast resort where he had been a leading light in the church choir, it was his first confrontation with strong language. At first his ears burned with shame, but his sensibilities soon became hardened. Returning home for week-end leave, he was seated at table when he noticed something vital was missing from his plate. Turning to his mother, politely he asked her to 'pass the f— HP Sauce'. For a few agonising moments, a truly dreadful silence reigned. Then his parents resumed their innocent conversation and the incident was never mentioned again.

In 1952 George VI died and his elder daughter Elizabeth succeeded to the throne. Large numbers of her subjects lined the streets of London to watch her coronation procession. Others viewed it on television sets enclosed in elongated cabinets of a rare unattractiveness. The concept of a New Elizabethan Age was launched, and the shade of Francis Drake evoked.

Gör som jag
sätt piff på
biff
köttbullar
pytt I panna
och korv
med
HP SÅS
-de ä gott de!

Englands finaste kryddsås

On a more mundane level, *Woman's Own* celebrated the end of egg rationing with an eight-page supplement. Advertisements and photographs that accompanied recipes began to appear in colour. Meat and canned foods became easier to obtain and one joyful day in 1954 the end of food rationing was announced.

HP Sauce Ltd did not remain unaffected by national developments. With the return of dried fruits to the market, their much-needed supplies of dates were now assured. Building plans for new laboratories were drawn up and Norfolk Canneries were acquired to package products such as baked beans, which bore the reassuring symbol of the famous Sauce.

At the beginning of 1950 the overseas markets of the Commonwealth countries and Scandinavia were as healthy as ever. The movement of British troops can always be traced by the exports of HP Sauce and sales at this time were large to Malta, Gibraltar, Bahrain, Aden, Port Said and West Germany. But at home and abroad a generation was growing up who had been born during a time when HP was considered a luxury item. No time was to be lost in developing their taste for this national delicacy and an army of salesmen were despatched throughout the length and breadth of the country.

The life of a salesman in the 1950s was markedly different to that of his equivalent today. A Homburg hat, stiff white collar and, above all, black shoes, were his uniform. Heaven help the hapless fellow who set forth in brown footwear! By 1958 the management in their wisdom decided that cars used by the sales force should be equipped with heaters. This only applied, however, to those travelling north of Manchester, the climate to the south of this being considered too mild for such a wild extravagance. Vast supermarkets were not yet the order of the day, and many a salesman had to move 'the cat off the bread' in the friendlier if less hygienic corner shop.

In 1957 the entire sales force basked in the light of reflected glory. Aston Villa Football team was captained by the brother of one of their number. This was the year when Villa won the Cup. Need more be said?

Disasters as well as triumphs hit those then working at HP. On an international scale events leading up to the 1956 Anglo-French invasion of Suez caused great concern to the management. The closing of the Suez Canal would mean both alternative suppliers and other supply routes would have to be found for certain raw materials.

At home another event of a liquid nature occurred just after Christmas 1956. One of the old maturing vats used in the vinegar-making process at HP decided to end its life in a truly spectacular fashion with a great explosion and a river of 45,000 gallons of malt vinegar started to roar its way down Tower Road. Cellars were flooded, three-piece suites floated in front parlours, fountains of vinegar gushed out of the plug holes of sinks and basins, and the cries of helpless householders rang from bedroom windows. For a quarter of a mile the mighty river ran its relentless course. The fire brigade worked hard with their pumps for three hours and the residents with their mops for even longer before some sort of order was achieved. But all efforts were unavailing against one result of the flood. THE SMELL!! 'We know it's fish and chips night but enough is enough', protested one despairing gentleman. HP promptly compensated the householders for the losses incurred, even if they were a little taken aback at the number of mink coats and family heirlooms apparently destroyed by the flooding of these humble buildings.

The excitement over and the small houses spick and span once more, it was back to the job of persuading the country that 'Everything goes with HP Sauce'. This slogan appeared on advertisements showing a bottle of the Sauce set against a background of a plate of succulent gammon or sizzling bacon and eggs. Photographed in colour, they appear rather cholesterol-ridden and unimaginative today, although the quantity of food displayed must have been a welcome sight after years of austerity. A 'Happy Families' campaign was run featuring such radio stars as Ben Lyon, Ted Ray, Charlie Chester and Alfred Marks with their respective families. Even the family dog appears greatly pleased by the presence of HP Sauce in these smiling groups.

It is a sign of the times that some of these advertisements also began to appear with pictures of stars of the newer medium, television. Terry Hall with Lennie the Lion and Hylda Baker with Cynthia ('She knows, yer know') now extolled the virtues of the Sauce. In 1958, not to be left behind by the advent of commercial television, HP began to screen a series of cartoon adver-

Bebe, Ben, Barbara and Richard Lyon say:

Everything goes with **HP** Sauce

"Aye, there's nothing left when there's a bottle of
HP Sauce on the table. You mark my words!"

... and Aggie will tell you that they also enjoy HP Tomato Ketchup and HP Baked Beans   They're so **Rich** in Tomato

Cynthia doesn't say.

Hylda Baker says:
That's our Cynthia up there
with the bottle of H.P. Sauce.
She doesn't say much, but
she knows, you know!
She knows that everything goes with H.P. Sauce.
She knows that H.P. Ketchup is so rich
in tomato. And she knows I know she knows
there's nothing like H.P. on the table
to make us a really . . .

Ha**pp**y **P**air!

She knows, you know!

Do you know the head of this

Ha**P**PY FAMILY

"When I praise H.P. Sauce, I speak
for everyone!" says "the voice
of them all." Yes, it's the famous
impersonator, Peter Cavanagh,
enjoying a picnic with his wife,
Joyce, and Roger, Anita and
Jennifer. As for Rex, well . . . he
leads a dog's life. No left-overs
when H.P. Sauce is about!

Everything
goes with

SoLuTioNS

PICTURE QUIZ

1. (c) **2.** (a) **3.** (b) **4.** (b) **5.** Never!
6. They drop at the same speed, will reach the floor together.

WHAT ARE THE·Y

1. HP Sauce Bottle from directly overhead. **2.** Rugger ball end-on.
3. Electric light bulb end-on, fitting foremost. **4.** Teacup seen from above. **5.** Dead front view of a toy railway engine. **6.** One roller skate seen from immediately below. **7.** Thick book lying open halfway seen at eye-level. **8.** Overhead view of teapot.

TRANSATLANTIC QUIZ

American	*English*
1. Baby Carriage	Pram (short for Perambulator)
2. Elevator	Lift
3. Sidewalk	Pavement
4. Subway	Tube
5. Vest	Waistcoat
6. Gasolene	Petrol
7. Rubbers	Galoshes

FLAGS OF THE NATIONS

1. U.S.A. **4.** South Africa **7.** Denmark **10.** Finland
2. France **5.** Iraq **8.** India **11.** Sudan
3. New Zealand **6.** Sweden **9.** Burma **12.** Egypt

IN THE TOYSHOP

The Picture contained the following objects :
Shopkeeper, Helicopter, Hoop, Ship, Sheep, Shepherd
Airship, Hospital, Grasshopper, Hippo, Whip
Chimpanzee, Sheepdog, Whippet, Hamper.

PICTURE CROSSWORD

ACROSS
1. Tomatoes **5.** Sauce **6.** Sty
8. Tee **11.** Dates **12.** Spaniels

DOWN
1. Tusk **2.** Mouse **3.** Ties **4.** Easy
7. Title **8.** Trap **9.** Eden **10.** Asps

Printed in England

A person would hear Big Ben quicker by Radio

tisements. One of them was an updated version of the famous pre-war poster portraying a disconsolate mongrel gazing with dismay at his master's empty plate.

By the end of the Fifties, the economy of the country generally was booming, and the standard of living had risen considerably. 'You've never had it so good', said Premier Harold Macmillan. With increased spending power, people began to seek ways of making their life an easier and pleasanter one. For many people taking a holiday became a possibility for the first time in their lives. For some this meant holiday camps in British resorts, but a visit abroad was becoming a reality for many others. This, combined with Britain's increasing imports of foreign foods, was leading to a growing interest in the cookery of other countries. Recipes for pizzas and spaghetti bolognaise began to appear in women's magazines.

HP Sauce had always been associated with such traditional English foods as hams, pork pies, sausages, bacon and fried fish. Some effort was now made to give it a more international image. One advertisement rather tentatively suggested the use of HP Sauce with risotto and a recipe for a curry was published, listing the sauce as one of its ingredients. (This later had a certain aptness as HP was a direct descendant of the hot sauces and chutneys brought to this country from India.) But it was apparent that the Sixties would be a testing and challenging period for the country's most famous brown sauce.

opposite *Page from a book of puzzles produced by HP Sauce*

Harold Wilson at the Midland Vinegar Company's centenary dinner, 1975

Hitting a century

'If Harold has a fault, it is that he will drown everything with HP Sauce'. Attributed to Mary Wilson.

The popular images of the so-called Swinging Sixties are those of the mini-skirt, Carnaby Street, Mary Quant, Vidal Sassoon and four young Liverpudlians called the Beatles. It was a time when the voice of the redbrick university was heard throughout the land, and the accents of the North became more fashionable than those of the Home Counties. By many it is recalled with nostalgia as a time of excitement and innovation. On the political scene, Harold Macmillan was obliged to resign, after a messy call-girl scandal involving one of his ministers, John Profumo. The 14th Earl of Home renounced his ancient title and as the humble Sir Alec Douglas Home succeeded as Prime Minister. His occupation of the position was brief, however. In 1964 a Labour government was elected, led by Harold Wilson. In their modest fashion, for HP Sauce and its birthplace, it would also be a period of profound changes.

At the beginning of the decade, HP produced a series of advertisements for the small screen, in which military types in dinner jackets extolled the virtues of the product. These seemed

quaintly old-fashioned and were soon replaced by commercials
where HP was recommended not only with such traditional
favourites as fried fish or shepherd's pie but with the more recently popular spaghetti and hamburger. The changing pattern of
the nation's eating habits was also reflected on the printed paper.
An advertisement in an issue of *Woman* magazine in 1963 for
'good old English HP' suggesting 'six traditional ways with Beef
and HP' was soon followed by another headed 'six Continental
ways with Chicken and HP'. Readers were encouraged not only
to use HP for 'Saucing up Sausages' or 'Shaking all over Fish
and Chips', but also to add it as a vital ingredient of several given
recipes. These included a 'Continental' Lamb Stew, and
something rather courageously described as 'Cod Portugaise'.

To back up these advertising campaigns, the sales force at HP were being instructed in new selling techniques. Their hairstyles, although nothing resembling those of the pop groups and 'flower-power' people that caused much apoplexy among the colonels of Cheltenham, were no more of the short back and sides variety. The Homburg hat was disappearing and the tailoring of their suits began to owe more to the influence of Italy than to those of Savile Row or the Fifty Shilling Tailors. (Not that those changes appealed to everyone. One Scots shopkeeper was so enraged by the 'hard sell' technique of one of this new breed of immaculate fast-talking salesmen that he chased the unfortunate young man out of his shop and pursued him down the main street brandishing a bacon knife.)

But invaluable as the efforts of the advertising agents and salesmen were, the effects of these were nothing compared to a remark casually made by one of the new occupants of No.10 Downing Street.

Harold Wilson had become Prime Minister after the Labour Party's victory in the 1964 General Election. His wife Mary was a pleasant-looking lady with a penchant for writing poetry. During an interview, shortly after her husband's accession to power, she complained gently about his habit of covering everything she cooked with HP Sauce. As she herself later said, 'My innocent remark was a quotation from Heaven for Peter Cook and Dudley Moore.' Indeed all the young satirists of the time leapt upon the statement with glee. Delightedly, they broadcast other supposed innovations introduced by the Wilsons to the dignified atmosphere of No.10. It was whispered that a certain tonic wine was sipped within its elegant walls, themselves newly decorated with plaster flying ducks. Doughty Tory matrons, often the victims of these young men's wit, laughed heartily and discreetly moved their own bottles of HP Sauce and Wincarnis to the back of their store cupboards.

Unperturbed, the Prime Minister puffed placidly at his pipe, neither confirming nor denying these stories. The impression gathered mainly from the slant of its own advertising was that HP was largely a working-class taste. If therefore the belief that he was devoted to the Sauce established his credentials as a man of the people, so be it. As for HP Sauce itself, not only was it receiving publicity on a scale undreamed of by its advertising agents, but its links with Parliament were now incontrovertible.

The Sauce received further inadvertent publicity at about the same period from the late lamented Marty Feldman. The pop-eyed comedian was making a long-playing record and wished to include a song in the French style with lyrics in that language. Denis King, the composer, imparted this news to the lyric-writer, actor John Junkin, who — remembering his lack of prowess in French from his schooldays — paled at the thought. However, inspiration alighted on his shoulders and, returning from his local grocer's with a bottle of HP Sauce, presented it to Marty with the suggestion that the French label could provide the lyric. The idea met with great approval, and Marty Feldman sang the famous words in his best Charles Aznavour style, under the title of 'La Sauce HP'.

HP by now lent its name to a variety of products, including tomato ketchup, baked beans and pickles. If perhaps regarded as a little old-fashioned, it was a firm nevertheless respected for the quality of the goods it produced. The giant Imperial Tobacco Company wished to diversify into the food market and made HP Sauce Ltd an offer for its shares. It was an offer they couldn't refuse and so in 1967 a famous British name was acquired by a huge multinational. Temporary buildings were erected at the Aston factory to house the swarms of marketing men who descended, eager to exploit even further the power of the HP label. In 1969 the directors of HP, with large sales and marketing departments, were transferred to a new centre of power, the attractive Regency town of Leamington Spa.

Left behind in the less genteel atmosphere of Aston were the works manager and staff, the chemists and a workforce bemused not only by changes in their working environment but by those in the locality generally. During the Fifties, many terraces of small houses in Aston had been demolished as part of a slum clearance programme. Now in the late Sixties, Birmingham embarked upon building its notorious roadway system. The remaining houses in Aston, homes of the majority of the HP workforce, fell victims to the bulldozers. Gone forever was the cookshop on the corner where cow heel could be purchased, the harness makers, and the small front parlour where the lady of the house had sold tea-leaves and milk to the HP girls for their forbidden cups of tea during the First World War. The former tight-knit community was now dispersed and moved to housing estates with well-deserved modern conveniences. HP had one small victory over the road makers, however. In the days of Samson Moore, a main had been laid underground to pump vinegar from the brewery to the maturing vats. When the land surrounding it was sunk for the motorway, HP insisted that the main remained intact. Today, encased in its own footbridge it is the only vinegar main to cross a motorway (nervous motorists may take comfort from engineers' assurances that the contents are unlikely ever to douse the unsuspecting travellers beneath it).

Towards the end of the Sixties, HP was involved with disruption on an international scale. In 1965, Rhodesia, unable to agree terms with Britain on a form of independence that would guard the rights of the black majority, made its own Unilateral Declaration of Independence, more commonly called UDI. Britain refused to recognise the new regime and imposed sanctions on all trade between the two countries. Rhodesia had been a good market for HP Sauce and its citizens began to bemoan its absence. Seizing his opportunity, some crafty entrepreneur began to market a sauce labelled RHP, with the bold, but untruthful declaration on the bottle that it was made 'under licence'. The British Foreign Office exploded at this news, but HP was easily able to prove its innocence in the matter. The company was, however, unable to take the rascally Rhodesian to court, as the regime under which he operated was held to be illegal. As a small gesture of repentance, the villain did substitute a picture of the Victoria Falls for that of the Houses of Parliament on his bottles.

In 1972 HP was amalgamated with another company within the Imperial Food empire, Smedleys of canned food fame. At the offices of the new company, Smedley HP Foods Ltd, at Leamington Spa, new schemes were endlessly devised to 'up-date' the marketing of the product. To meet the growing taste for a blander sauce, they introduced a 'Fruity' version of HP. They also had to face the challenge of the greater variety now apparent in the British diet. Immigration had firmly established the popularity of Asian restaurants and their invaluable take-away service. The large number of people holidaying abroad had led to an increasing interest in other European cuisines. No good advertising man would dream of patronising anything but the ubiquitous Italian *trattoria* and recipe books filled with ideas from France, Spain, Greece etc, poured hot from the press every day.

Attempts were made to fit HP into these Continental habits of eating. One such was a television commercial, made by now of course in colour, with a rather unlikely scenario. This depicted a family of English tourists seated out of doors at a small French café. The meal in front of them appears delicious, but by the look on their faces something seems to be lacking. Hey Presto! From nowhere the father of the family produces a bottle of HP Sauce. Every member of the family pours a generous measure of the contents onto his plate and the meal is then eaten with enthusiasm. Watching this strange ritual from nearby tables are the native French. (One can tell they're French as the men are all dressed in striped jerseys and black berets.) The kindly English, noticing the interest on their faces, invite them to sample their bottle. This is done with much trepidation but the result is pronounced '*magnifique*' with many suitably Gallic gestures. (An advertisement one feels aimed at the more cosmopolitan of the British rather than the French who have never developed an appreciation of our 'thicker' sauces.)

1975 was a remarkable year for HP. Disquieting rumours had been heard that the management intended to close down the factory at Aston Cross. But at the beginning of the year Imperial Foods dispelled fears by announcing that, on the contrary, they were to spend £1 million pounds on expanding and modernising the premises. Indeed demand for the Sauce was high, and the relieved workforce, not all of whom had taken kindly to the new and rather faceless style of management, applied themselves energetically to the task of meeting new orders. But HP had another cause for celebration, for it was now a hundred years since that shrewd and energetic young man, Edwin Samson Moore, had established his Midland Vinegar Company at Aston Cross.

To mark the occasion a great banquet was arranged to be attended by 200 distinguished guests. Most notable of these would be that much publicised devotee of HP Sauce, Harold Wilson. On the evening appointed, the guests arrived to find the

HP Sauce Limited

festive tables laid with shining cutlery, sparkling glasses and miniature replicas of the original Garton's bottle, one per person. Good wine was quaffed and good food enjoyed, including the aptly named savoury 'La Croute aux Oeufs Sauce HP'. An atmosphere of well-being and justifiable pride prevailed when the Prime Minister stood up to speak.

After expressing congratulations to the company and urging it to further efforts in the export market, Mr Wilson paused. He then made a confession, which astounded the assembled company. Contrary to popular belief, it was not HP but Worcestershire Sauce for which he had a marked partiality. Poor HP Sauce, even at such a moment, to be outshone by its social superior!

But the thick brown sauce has a habit of disconcerting its severest critics. On this occasion its champion was the Chairman of Imperial Foods. In his speech of reply he predicted that HP Sauce would still be on our tables in 2075 and gently reminded Harold Wilson that it had so far survived nineteen Prime Ministers who were in office twenty-seven times. He then added 'it is tempting to reflect that there has been rather more change in British politics than there has been in our product'. Harold Wilson, currently leading a minority Labour government, no doubt took the point.

Five sauce bottles. from left to right *Labelled HP Sauce bottle showing glass stopper with cork surround, produced 1917; HP Sauce bottle produced 1947 showing post-war economy label; HP Sauce bottle (liberated by British Task Force in May 1982 from chef's kitchen in disused whaling station, South Georgia, Falkland Islands);*
HP Fruity Sauce bottle (launched in 1971) with metal cap; current HP Sauce bottle, 1983

Onwards and for ever

'Epicurean cooks sharpen with cloyless sauce his appetite.'
Shakespeare, *Antony and Cleopatra*

There have been further changes on the political scene since that celebrated dinner of 1975. The following year Harold Wilson resigned as Prime Minister and it is tempting to wonder whether that most chameleon-like of politicians had chosen Worcestershire Sauce as a taste more befitting an elder statesman and future peer of the realm that the humbler HP. He was succeeded by 'Uncle Jim' Callaghan. In 1979 the Conservatives were returned to power, led by Britain's first woman Prime Minister, the redoubtable Margaret Thatcher, who declared war on inflation, but in 1982 found herself with another battle on her hands when Argentina invaded the Falkland Islands.

Towards the end of this conflict, HP Sauce made a surprising appearance on the battle field. While in the process of liberating South Georgia, a detachment of the British Task Force came across a disused whaling station. Even in this bleak and apparently deserted landscape they approached the building with great caution. Eventually on their bursting open the door, the sight that met their astonished eyes caused them to stop in mid-attack. Confronting them were no Argentine guerillas but two bottles of HP Sauce placed upon a kitchen table. They had been left behind when the station was abandoned in 1946 and the contents were in perfect condition. These bottles were borne back in triumph to Britain by the victorious soldiers. Today they occupy pride of place in HP's headquarters.

HP Sauce is still held in great affection in Britain. During filming on location of *A Passage to India*, the catering contractors kept the British cast and crew happy with supplies of their favourite foods. These included meat and fish pastes, baked beans, tinned sardines, sausages and, of course, bottles of HP Sauce.

Deep-sea diver and treasure hunter, Richard Knight, was recently released from a Vietnamese jail, where he had spent fourteen months for allegedly infringing territorial waters. On arrival home in Britain, he declared to the press his intention of trying to forget this rather uncomfortable experience and concentrate instead on the immediate pleasures of 'a cup of tea, a pint of beer, baked beans on toast, fish and chips and HP Sauce'.

Godfrey Smith composing a list of things quintessentially English for *The Sunday Times* of 12 August 1984 included it amongst the royal family, cottages, darts, xenophobia and the *Oxford English Dictionary*. *The Observer* in the same year, offering ninety-nine reasons for feeling glad to be British, included HP Sauce amongst, to mention a few, the Grand National, *Private Eye*, pantomime dames, the Loch Ness monster, crumpets, Quentin Crisp, jumble sales, kippers, cathedrals and dogs.

As well as featuring on the printed page, the bottle has also in its modest way become a celebrity of the small screen. Frequently glimpsed in our most famous soap opera *Coronation Street*, it was recently overcome by the honour of appearing with the divine Judi Dench in *A Fine Romance*. Mel Smith and Griff Rhys Jones, talented performers and writers, have appeared as two disgruntled bluebottles settled atop a giant HP bottle.

It recently proved both medium and inspiration for an exhibit at the International Contemporary Art Fair. David Mach called his sculpture, which depicted a woman lying on her back against the Union Jack, 'Thinking of England'. This witty sexual joke was made from 1,800 HP Sauce bottles.

top *HP Sauce shares the screen with Judi Dench
and Michael Williams*
below *David Mach with his sculpture*

A private education
Is not just Os and As
But constant deprivation
Of bottled mayonnaise;
For how can a Sloane Ranger
Aspire to pass the course,
Unless she learns the danger
Of eating HP Sauce?

This little verse submitted by the Bursar of the exclusive Malvern Girls' College shows that, if the pungent brown Sauce retains its hold on Britain's affection, its image in this class-conscious country still remains a little less than aristocratic. One can admit to buying one's underwear from 'Marks' (and Spencer don't y' know) or one's groceries from J. Sainsbury with impunity. But declare a liking for HP Sauce and a small tight smile of amused condescension is often the reaction.

Perhaps the rather unsophisticated nature of the foods associated with it and the style of its advertisements have been responsible for this. Perhaps also it was originally believed that its presence denoted that one had neither the time, money nor domestic help necessary to produce one's own sauces or pickles.

However, the following information culled from the bastions of privilege reveals the attitude still held towards the product in certain quarters. Fortnum and Mason, that glittering emporium of epicurean delights, did admit reluctantly, when we asked them, to stocking the Sauce and further admitted that over the decades there had been the occasional request for its inclusion in one of their famous hampers. The word 'occasional', however, was heavily stressed. Harrods cheerfully revealed that they sold what they described as 'the best of brown sauces'. Their representative did however lower his voice to impart the information that it was also available in their restaurant, but only when requested and NEVER appeared on the table.

Among the gentlemen's clubs it appeared that the Sauce is never used at the Athenaeum and, as far as can be ascertained, never has been, while Whites froze the blood with their statement, 'we do not use bottled sauce'. At the Army and Navy the consumption is minimal and a representative of the Cavalry and

Guards Club stated in best parade-ground fashion: 'those people who find it necessary to add a *sauce of this nature** sometimes ask for Cumberland sauce, but we feel we can say with some assurance that most members shun the use of HP Sauce!' (Strong words indeed, but somewhat mitigated by the information that in an area known as 'the snack bar' some members *do* use HP Sauce with their 'bangers and mash'.)

Claridges Hotel was emphatic that there had never been any demand for the Sauce at that prestigious establishment, adding, 'The reason could be that we make our own sauces according to the tradition of the French cuisine', and The Ritz also insisted all its sauces were freshly made. (One feels both institutions, in the flush of gastronomic pride rather missed the point. Do their renowned chefs themselves really produce some piquant little number to enhance one's breakfast tray?) The Dorchester does have, as they put it, 'that famous British Institution' hidden in decent obscurity, in their Grill Room, in order to fulfil the infrequent order. At the Savoy their only demand for HP Sauce comes from 'elderly English clients and then *only* with breakfast'.

At one-time Simpsons in the Strand, that most English of restaurants, would have had that most English of sauces on service with other condiments. Indeed the Master Cook has memories of 'a very, very distinguished regular customer from the Law Courts who had his own inscribed condiment set and if the Commis Waiter omitted his HP Sauce all hell was let loose'. A rare occurrence that made the staff fear for the fate of those appearing before his Lordship later that afternoon. But the predilections of legal luminaries counted for nothing and about twenty years ago the powers that be at Simpsons decreed 'that any item with a "Trade Name" be removed from open view'. So even here among the best of British beef, sausages and hams, HP's traditional partners, the Sauce is kept discreetly in the background.

The attitudes of other countries towards HP Sauce are far less complex. They either love it or hate it, and a great many of them love it. The Scandinavian countries are still faithful customers. The ubiquitous presence of the meatball in Sweden and the prevalence of potato in the Danish diet may explain their partiality.

* Author's italics.

Demand from Britain's former colonies is still strong. And let us not imagine that the presence of the Sauce in sunny Spain is solely due to the necessity of making the British tourist feel at home. Since the opening of the Spanish + Gibraltar border, Spaniards have been swarming through the gates to stock up with British 'delicacies', HP Sauce amongst them.

The newest and most enthusiastic of customers are to be found in the oil-rich sheikdoms of the Middle East. Indeed such is its prestige in those countries that as a natural compliment it was placed before our Gracious Queen at a banquet during a recent Royal Tour of Saudi Arabia. HP Sauce is in fact legally obtainable in over 113 different countries with the labels on the bottles translated into many different languages. Its clandestine presence has been discovered by relieved HP lovers in other countries too. A bottle was spotted at the Nile Hilton, which, as Egypt has placed an embargo on the Sauce, was certainly smuggled. Pakistan also, anxious to encourage its own products, has banned its importation. Nevertheless, supplied by ships from Singapore, it has been found on certain stalls selling briskly for £1.15 a bottle.

The Sauce has also been paid the compliment of dubious imitation all over the world. Although the labels of these have borne a passing similarity to that of the genuine article, the contents have proved a different story.

ut one sad fact remains among the euphoric tales of inter-
ati 1al approval. France, home of *haute cuisine*, has never
cap 1lated to the charms of HP Sauce. Lea and Perrins
Wo estershire, has won its seal of approval, but HP never!
Inde d it is rumoured that one Frenchman, after an initial sampl-
ing, sped with shock and declared that in his opinion it should
be ore justly described as 'une sauce incendiaire'!

ut if the Sauce's devotees at home and abroad have remained
co ant, there have been dramatic changes in its production and
pi entation during the past few years. HP, under the giant
u rella of Imperial Foods, has now been divorced from
S dleys and has a new partner in Golden Wonder. This firm,
w -known for its potato crisps, also manufactures those pots
of ehydrated pasta which with the addition of boiling water are
t ned into the ad man's dream of a housewife's lunch. The head-
arters of HP Foods are based in Market Harborough, a plea-
ant Leicestershire market town. Here are to be found the
managing director, export manager, sales managers, in fact, every
sort of manager you can think of. Occasionally these bright-witted
men take time off from making important decisions and climb
into their cars to make the hour's drive to Aston Cross. Here,
descending like the gods from Olympus, they leave the motorway to reach ground level.

The scene that meets their eyes is one of apparent devasta-
tion. Builders' dust fills the air and cranes and bulldozers are
busily employed in the process of giving the Sauce factory a multi-
million pound face-lift. Inside 'The Sauce' the atmosphere has
a true 'works' feeling as friendly Brummies, both black and white,
go about their everyday jobs. Their task is to produce the product about which such momentous decisions are taken in distant Market Harborough. Great changes are to take place in their
environment. New bottling plants and loading bays are to be
erected, and splendidly modern offices provided for the works
manager and his staff.

The old Vulcan Brewery purchased by Samson Moore in
1902 has already disappeared. The old brewery where he
established the Midland Vinegar Company, cornerstone of his
fortunes, is due for destruction as is the curious vinegar main
crossing the motorway. However, at Aston Cross one thing

remains constant. Drive past the factory with any local and his nose will rise in the air and, sniffing appreciatively, he will proclaim 'brewing at "The Sauce" today'!

While the workforce at Aston get on with the job of ensuring supplies of 'the best-known and most popular thick sauce in the world', the marketing men in far away offices are conferring with the men from the advertising agency. Their job is to find new, and, they hope, better, ways of promoting HP. In the late 1970s television commercials still showed HP associated with such traditional foods as Bubble and Squeak, York Ham and Pork Pie. Nowadays a discreetly 'punk' young man is shown being roused from a catatonic state into a frenzy of delight by the addition of HP Sauce to his hamburger.

A campaign of the early 1980s produced ripples of disapproval. These were cartoon commercials based on the suggestive seaside postcards of Donald McGill and featured one 'Arthur' fancying a 'bit on the side'. (A bit of HP Sauce on the side of his plate, of course). Several reverend gentlemen complained 'at the lowering of moral standards by such an old-established company', however, and the campaign was withdrawn.

But their reaction was as nothing compared to that created by a more recent attempt to 'update' the Sauce. Anger and apoplexy abounded when it was discovered in the autumn of 1984 that the French paragraph on which so many of us had cut our linguistic teeth had disappeared without trace from the label on the HP Sauce bottle. Letters of alarm and despondency filled the correspondence columns of *The Times*.

'What does this portend?' cried one anguished correspondent in tones that suggested the imminent collapse of our national way of life.

A doctor from the West Country anxiously enquired 'Am I alone among your readers in deploring the loss of that much loved and most piquant of French primers — the label on the HP Sauce bottle?'

Indeed he was not. Another correspondent assured him, 'There must be many who miss the opportunity to polish up their Français by constant study of the description of the virtues of HP Sauce.'

The loss was also regretted by another because 'It used to

"FANCY A BIT ON THE SIDE?"

You've got to admire their Sauce.

You've got to admire HP's sauce: they're spending over a million from January on a provocative new campaign, full of cheeky seaside-postcard humour, that'll keep the unique taste of HP Sauce where it belongs – on every British table.

They'll go for bust!

A hilarious new cartoon series on TV will give HP a jaunty new image, boost sales of the other popular HP brands, and give an irresistible uplift to a couple of bouncy new products the development team are keeping close to their chests…

Shameless!

Hordes of customers will soon be after a bit on the side – so grocers who shamelessly show off the size of their HP stocks (and take advantage of that naughty profit margin) are in for a thrilling time!

contain the sentence "Elle est absolument pure", which I used in my French classes to teach my students that "it" in French was as likely to be "elle" as "il". They never forgot it.'

A lady from Yorkshire wrote that she had been inspired by the same words, 'elle est absolument pure' to lead a blameless childhood, with the result that she was now 'a Women's Institute President and all due to HP Sauce!'

'The French label must return' came the call from Scotland and 'you have breached the entente cordiale' were words flung at the head of the managing director of HP Foods.

The management admit to much soul-searching before launching this latest attempt in 'the constant process of adapting the image of this famous product to appeal to contemporary taste'. One hopes they achieve this but in the meantime they have not only alarmed the traditionalists but robbed us of a most endearing irony. A sauce bottle label written for a nation renowned for its lack of linguistic ability, in the language of the one country that can't abide the stuff!

So, denuded of its mourned French label, what are the challenges facing HP Sauce today? It is threatened by the Red Menace of Tomato Ketchup, which the burger generation seem to prefer, and soy sauce is the natural ally of the Yellow Peril of Chinese take-away. Encouraged to change our dietary habits, we are assured that 'high fibre is good for you' (little scope for HP here you might think, although many may consider that a drop of the Sauce could only improve the noxious bran). 'Cut down on your fats', say those that know best, thus condemning the sausages, hams and pies that HP has traditionally been served with. But, above all, it is the sad decline of the British breakfast that poses HP's biggest problem.

Health-conscious wives now present their husbands with a bowl whose contents seem more suitable for sowing in the garden than regarding as a serious foodstuff. Hotels advertise a Continental Breakfast, which all too often turns out to be a plate of cold toast not buttery French croissants. But here let us pause and raise our hats to British Rail. At a cost, they still provide a full and, to some, glorious, British breakfast and there is always a bottle of HP Sauce on the table.

After this roll call of dismal facts, let us not despair. In over eighty years of existence, HP Sauce has survived many changes in eating habits, withstood the scorn of snobs and resisted the disapproval of gourmets. It has outlived twenty-one Prime Ministers and provided solace during the dangerous and difficult years of two world wars. Over the decades it has become not only an old friend but something more. Let the last words rest with E.H. Moore, grandson of Samson Moore. Addressing the Editor of *The Times* during the furore caused by the change of label, he begins 'Sir, If HP Sauce is not already regarded universally as a national institution, surely the fact that it merits discussion in the correspondence columns of your famous newspaper finally confers on it this status.'

LA SAUCE HP

Lyrics by
JOHN JUNKIN

Music by
DENIS KING

Rubato

Cette sauce de haute qual-it-é est un mé-lang-e de fruits or-i-en-taux, d'é-pices et de vin-aig-re de 'Malt'. Elle est ab-so-lu-ment pure et ne con-tient au cun-e ma-tiè-re col-or-ante syn-the-tique ni au-cun a-gent de con-ser-va-tion art-i-fici-el. La Sauce H P est app-é-tiss-ant-e et dé-lic-ieuse av-ec viandes chaudes et froides, pois-son, jam-bon, from-age et sa-lade. Elle est é-gal-ment ex-cel-lent pour en-rich-ir le sa-veur des soupes, ha-chis, et rag-oûts. La Sauce H P Oh oh oh oh oh oh oh oh oh et av-ec pommes frites et de pois-son ge-fil-te.